Ketogenic

For Rapid Weight Loss And A Healthier Lifestyle

(2 weeks meal plan with 40 best easy & delicious keto vegetarian diet recipes)

By James Stone

JS Healthy Eating Publishing Limited

Table of Contents

Introduction

I would like to thank you and congratulate you for choosing this Ketogenic Vegetarian book!

In modern life, we are all want to have a healthier lifestyle. We want to be more slimmer, be more stronger, lose excess weight, be more confident, have better mood and better skin. We want to have good sleep, have more energy everyday, be more active, have less disease, etc. We want to be longevity, less pain, more happy thing.

But do you know how can you get these above good result? How will you have a better life? How can you be longevity and have less pain?

The answers you will find by following this book! This book is related to ketogenic vegetarian diet cookbook. It will tell you everything important you need to know about it. You will know why other people are more healthier, beautiful or handsome. You will know it is possible for you to have a better life without make too many changes. Your life will be more healthier!

We have helped at least 300,000 people lose their weight and get a better body state by this book foe the past 5 years. I believe you will also find the right answers just by reading this book and put it into action! You no need to pay much more time for other similar books, just stick to this one!

So what will you find in this book?

1. The ketogenic Diet and it's advantages

2. The Vegetarian Diet and it's benefits

3. What is Ketogenic Vegetarian Diet

4. Why we should follow Ketogenic Vegetarian Diet

5. What should we eat and what shouldn't eat when in ketogenic vegetarian diet

6. A 2-week meal plan guides you a successful ketogenic vegetarian diet

7. 40 delicious and Easy recipes support your long term diet journey

8. More and more...

All the recipes in the meal plan can be found on the recipe part of this book, and you can change the recipe to the similar one as you like, but the nutrition value should be no big difference to insure that you are still on the ketogenic vegetarian diet.

Meantime all the recipes in this book are very easy to follow, the ingredients are also easy to be found on the local market, which really will save you too much time. With the step by step procedure, you will know how to make all the recipes, even if you are a newer of cooking recipes, you can complete a very good flavored dish! You will not miss them!

For more information, please go on reading the rest of this book. Welcome to the ketogenic vegetarian diet world!

Best Wishes

James Stone

Chapter 1: The Ketogenic Diet

What is Ketogenic Diet?

The ketogenic diet also referred to as "keto" is a low carbohydrate high fat diet which causes the body to burn fat at an accelerated rate. It is an effective weight loss diet with many health benefits. When the diet is strictly followed, it will raise blood ketone levels which provides a new source of fuel for the body. Ketone is changed from fat, that means when you eat low carb high fat foods for a period, your body will get into a new state, which is called " KETOSIS", in which your body fat will be burned very quick. Meantime you will lose your weight fast than other diets.

When you consume foods that are high in carbohydrates, the body produces insulin and glucose. Then your body resource is mainly from carbohydrates, and when you eat many high carbs foods, your body cannot digest all of them, then they will transform to fat in your belly, thigh, hip, etc. until your body weight increases day by day. That's why we are fat.

- **Glucose:** The word glucose is derived from the Greek word for "sweet." It is a form of sugar that is used by the body for energy. As glucose is transported through the blood stream to the cells it is referred to as blood sugar or blood glucose.

- **Insulin:** Is a hormone responsible for transporting glucose to the blood into the cells for storage and energy.

There are different types of ketogenic diet, they are as follows:

- **Standard Ketogenic Diet:** This is the standard high carbohydrate, low fat diet.

- **Targeted Ketogenic Diet:** This is combined with the standard keto diet and consuming small amounts of fast digesting carbohydrates before a workout.

- **Cyclical Ketogenic Diet:** This version involves consuming an excessive amount of carbs three times, one day a week to resupply glycogen stores. This version is popular among bodybuilders and contest goers.

History and Current Size of Ketogenic Diet

The ketogenic diet grew in popularity during the 1920's and 1930's. The main purpose of the diet was as an alternative to fasting, which had proved beneficial for epilepsy patients. However, the diet was eventually discarded due to an influx of new epilepsy medication. The diet was re-introduced in 1994 after the parents of Charlie Abraham cured him of epilepsy using the ketogenic diet. They then began the Charlie Foundation which gave the diet media attention.

Weight loss is not the only reason people follow the keto diet. Many people follow it for medical reasons to cure some medical conditions, such as Alzheimer and Parkinson's disease. Bodybuilders and athletes use it to enhance muscle development and endurance.

How Your Body Works on Ketogenic Diet

The body goes through many biological changes when on a ketogenic diet; this includes an acceleration of fat breakdown, and a reduction of insulin. This causes the liver to produce large amounts of ketones in order to provide energy for the brain. This process is called ketosis and there are several things that will happen to the body during this time, these include:

- Bad breath
- Weight loss
- Appetite suppression
- Increased energy and focus
- Short term tiredness
- Constipation or diarrhoea
- Insomnia

The main aim of a keto diet that is properly maintained is to force the body into the metabolic state of ketosis. This is not achieved through eliminating calories but through the elimination of carbohydrates.

The human body is extremely adaptive and it will conform to whatever is put into it. When the body is starved of carbohydrates and overloaded with fats, it will start burning ketones as the primary source of energy. When the body reaches a high state of ketosis there are several performance, mental, and physical benefits.

Why you Should go on Ketogenic Diet

Here are some reasons why you should go on a ketogenic diet:

- **Brain Fuel:** When the body is in a ketosis state stronger fuel is pumped to the brain leading to an increase in energy and focus. This fuel also acts as a protection against neurological disorders.

- **Weight Loss Jump Start:** The ketogenic diet jump starts the weight loss process. Due to the lack of carbohydrates the body is forced to convert stored fat into energy for its fuel. Due to the drop in insulin levels, the body is transformed into a fat burning machine.

- **Prevents Oxidative Damage:** The ketogenic diet prevents further destruction of weak cells, as well as creating newer and stronger cells to fight off disease and infection.

Health Benefits of Ketogenic Diet

Ketogenic diet have been controversial according to some medical experts, stating such diets raise cholesterol and cause heart disease because they are high in fat. However, this opinion is now changing due to over 20 studies conducted on humans that prove the benefits of a Ketogenic diet. Here are some of those health benefits:

Increases HDL (good cholesterol)

HDL is responsible for carrying cholesterol away from the body towards the liver, so that it can either be excreted or reused. High levels of HDL can reduce the risk of heart disease.

Reduces Blood Sugar and Insulin Levels

Carbohydrates raise sugar levels in the body. Having high blood sugar level is toxic and causes insulin resistance which leads to type 2 diabetes. A reduction in carbohydrate consumption leads to lower blood sugar and insulin levels.

Weight Loss

Several studies have found that people on a low-carb diet lose more weight and lose it faster than those on a low-fat diet. This is due to low-carb diet eliminates excess water from the body. The kidneys also excrete excess sodium, which leads to quick weight loss during the first two weeks of being on the diet.

Mental Focus

Ketones provide fuel for the brain. When carbohydrates intake is reduced, it eliminates blood sugar spikes. Together this can improve concentration and focus. Studies have found that an increase in fatty acids can have a positive effect on the overall function of the brain.

Normalizes Hunger & Increases Energy

By providing your body with a more reliable source of energy, you will feel more energized throughout the day. When fats are burned as fuel they provide the body with the most energy. Fat is also more satisfying, which leaves us feeling satiated for a longer period of time.

Epilepsy Treatment

Although the ketogenic diet has only recently gained public attention, it has been used since the 1900's as a successful treatment for epilepsy. The diet continues to be one of the most widely used therapies to treat children with uncontrollable epilepsy.

Chapter 2: The Vegetarian Diet

What is Vegetarian Diet?

In general, a vegetarian diet excludes meat. However, this definition is too simplistic because there is more than one type of vegetarian diet, these include:

- **Lacto-ovo Vegetarian:** The word "lacto" means milk, and the word "ovo" means eggs. This type of vegetarian diet includes the consumption of eggs, yogurt, cheese, and milk products, but no fish, seafood, poultry, or meat.

- **Lacto-Vegetarian:** Includes the consumption of milk products but no fish, seafood, poultry, meat, or eggs.

- **Vegans:** They eat plant-based foods only, they don't consume any food that derives from animals. This includes gelatine, honey, eggs, and milk products.

Advantages of Vegetarian Diet

If you want to improve your health, a vegetarian diet is a step in the right direction. Vegetarians consume higher amounts of unsaturated fat, magnesium, Vitamins C and E, folic acid fiber and countless phytochemicals. This results in less risk of heart disease, vegetarians also have lower blood pressure and are slimmer. Here are some of the benefits of a vegetarian diet:

Improves Mood

Arachidonic acid comes from the dietary animal sources; research has found that there is a link between arachidonic acid and mood disorders. Researchers at Benedictine University found that when animal products were restricted the mood of the participant was better.

Reduces Risk of Obesity and Stroke

Due to vegetarians being particular about the food they choose to consume, they are less likely to binge eat due to their emotions, which is one of the main bad habits that contributes to obesity. Vegetarians are also less likely to suffer from strokes because they follow a diet that is low in cholesterol.

Reduces Risk of Cardiovascular Disease

Vegetarian diets are rich in antioxidants; antioxidants are responsible for reducing the damage caused by oxidative stress which minimizes the risk of cardiovascular disease.

Chapter 3: The Ketogenic Vegetarian Diet

What is Ketogenic Vegetarian Diet?

The ketogenic vegetarian diet is low carb, high fat diet that excludes meat. The traditional keto diet includes a lot of meat for protein. It is not a requirement to eat meat on the keto diet because one of the most important factors of the diet is fat, which you can get from vegetarian foods.

The ease in which vegetarians are capable of following a low carbohydrate diet is dependent upon how strict you are as a vegetarian. If you eat shellfish and fish, you won't have any problems. Oily fish such as tuna and salmon are fantastic options when it comes to a partial low carb vegetarian diet. If you eat dairy and eggs, you are in a much better position because you can make a lot of protein-rich satisfying meals with eggs such as crustless quiches and eggs.

Nuts are also a good ingredient for a low carb vegetarian diet because they are rich in nutrients, fats and oil. However, there must be a restriction imposed when eating them because they contain small amounts of carbohydrates.

Benefits of Ketogenic Vegetarian Diet

Although vegetarians tend to be slimmer than meat eaters, there are some who struggle with their weight. The typical vegetarian diet contains less fat and more carbs than the majority of meat-based diets. Some vegetarians find it difficult to process carbohydrates, which causes weight gain and other health problems. Therefore, one of the main benefits for the vegetarian on ketogenic diet is weight loss.

Each year the Center for Disease Control compiles a list of the leading cause of death in America. For several years, the killer at the top of the list has been heart disease as well as diabetes, Alzheimer's, accidents, strokes, respiratory problems, and cancer. Although none of these conditions appear to be related, most fall under the same umbrella of lifestyle diseases; this means making healthier lifestyle choices can prevent them.

This is why the majority of plant-based doctors recommend consuming a low fat vegetarian diet to prevent and reverse most chronic diseases. The Japanese consume a high carbohydrate diet, and are amongst the healthiest people in the world.

Research has discovered the fiber found in plant-based foods protects against heart disease. Whereas, it is the cholesterol found in animal foods responsible for heart related diseases. One meal containing animal products can paralyze the arteries; it also leads to temporary inflammation. If every meal we eat contains animal foods, we risk experiencing chronic inflammation that can harm our cardiovascular system, as well as our brain and lungs.

A ketogenic vegetarian diet can suppress cancer by 80% better than a diet where meat is consumed. Research has also found that meat eaters carry 2-3 more times the risk of developing Alzheimer's than those who consume a vegan or vegetarian diet.

A diet high in fiber helps to reduce diarrhoea, constipation as well as autoimmune diseases. You can also cure candida and acne through a low fat diet.

Do's and Don'ts for Successful Ketogenic Vegetarian Journey

Do be careful with your protein and carb choices because traditional vegetarian types of protein include grains and beans, which are not part of a keto diet.

Do consume more low carb vegetables, this will provide bulk and fiber to ensure that you get enough to eat.

Do limit your fruit intake and only stick to those that are low in carbohydrates and sugar, such as:

- Blackberries
- Strawberries
- Raspberries
- Blueberries

Don't be afraid to try new vegetables and cook them in different ways, especially if you are not a fan of raw food. You can try cooking some in butter or coconut oil.

Don't consume packaged vegetarian and vegan meat substitutes. The majority of them contain a high carbohydrate content.

Don't eat any genetically modified or non-fermented soy products.

Foods That Should be on Your Plate:

- Legumes and beans
- Tofu
- Tempeh
- Vegetable and soy protein powder
- Meatless sausages and bacon
- Sandwich slices
- Fish substitutes
- Chicken substitutes
- Soy burgers
- Vegetable and tofu dogs
- Seitan
- Salt and pepper

- Blended seasoning
- Worcestershire sauce
- Soy sauce
- Assorted spices and herbs
- Siracha sauce
- Mustard
- Soy mayonnaise
- Extra virgin olive oil
- Canola oil
- Grapeseed oil
- Peanut oil
- Coconut oil
- Palm shortening
- Assorted vinegars
- Soy flour
- Whole grain bread
- Splenda
- Soy milk
- Olive, nut, and avocado butters
- Popcorn
- Nuts
- Fruits
- Vegetables

Foods That Shouldn't be on Your Plate:

- White pasta
- White rice
- White bread
- Cereals with low fiber and added sugar
- Non diet sodas
- Carrots (high carb vegetable)
- Corn (high carb vegetable)
- Sweet potatoes (high carb vegetable)
- Yams (high carb vegetable)
- Potatoes (high carb vegetable)
- Fruit juices
- Chips
- Tortillas
- Crackers
- Pretzels

You can top your food with a natural sweetener but because they are processed make sure you use them sparingly. You can also spice up your food with a combination of herbs and salt, but just make sure your sodium intake is limited to 1,000 mg per day.

Foods such as olives, tofu, avocadoes, seeds, and nuts should be eaten in moderation. No more than 15 to 20 percent of your calories should come from these sources.

Everyone has different preferences and needs so experiment with different amounts to find out what suits your needs. You should greatly reduce or cut out oil completely from your diet.

Other Lifestyle Factors

There are several lifestyle suggestions that come with ketogenic vegetarian diet in order to reap the full benefits:

Sleep: Everyone needs rest, it's an essential process which enables the body to digest, recover, and heal. Adults require a minimum of 8 hours sleep per day; however, those on a high carb diet require between 9-10 hours sleep per day, going to bed by 10pm and waking up at 7am.

Hydration: It is essential that you drink enough water to maintain good health. It is recommended that adults consume 8, 8 ounce glasses, or half a gallon, of water per day. However, those on a ketogenic vegetarian diet should consume between 1 - 1 1/2 gallons of water per day despite consuming more water-based foods. You should make a conscience effort of drinking water throughout the day.

Exercise: There is an increased drive to be more active when excess sugar is flowing through the body. You will often see high carb eaters riding their bike, or running for several hours through the week. They typically work out every day and sometimes twice per day. While it isn't a necessary requirement that we exercise twice per day, you might want to intensify your work out regime in the beginning of your lifestyle change to weight loss but remember to be careful. Overexerting your body can also result in medical issues; such as dehydration, extreme weight loss that does not last.

Calories: Experts have continuously disagreed with the average daily calorie intake amount. The suggestion is between 1,800 – 2,000 calories for women, and 2,500 calories for men. The numbers are completely different for those on a ketogenic vegetarian diet. You are required to consume a minimum of 2,500 – 3,000 calories per day, and eating as much as 6,000 calories when you are extremely active.

Chapter 4: Epic Vegetarian Diet Meal Plan

Week 1 & 2 Shopping List

Eggs	Organic lemons	Coconut flour
Almond flour	Red cabbage	Carrots
Ground almonds	Medium beets	Vanilla extract
Zucchinis	Swiss chard	Unsweetened almond milk
Grated Parmigiano-Reggiano	Red pepper flakes	Ground ginger
Dried oregano	Artichokes	Gelatin
Salt	Broccoli	Butter
Pepper	Grated Parmesan	Strawberries
Soft cream	Bok choy	Any liquid

cheese		sweetener
Flax meal	Fresh green asparagus	Ground mustard seeds
Ground cinnamon	Medium artichokes	Shaved parmesan
Mint leaves	Green onions	Hot sauce
Olive oil	Ground white pepper	Black seedless olives
Ground flaxseed	Eggplant	Vegetarian broth
Gluten free baking powder	Garlic powder	Red bell peppers
Sea salt	Sweet potatoes	Dill
Coconut oil	Kale	Himalayan rock salt
Sage	Arugula	Yellow onion
Cilantro	Coconut milk	White mushrooms

Parsley	Ground nutmeg	Red onions
Basil	Seasoning of your choice	Tomatoes
Cauliflower	Cremini mushrooms	Cucumber
Mozzarella cheese	Unsweetened tomatoes	Celery
Garlic	Ghee	Tomato juice
Oregano	Ground cardamom	White wine vinegar
Millet flour	Shallots	White stevia
Tapioca flour	Fresh green beans	Croutons
Baking powder	Capers	Onion powder
Milk	Italian parsley	Avocado
Leeks	Sweet paprika	Soy seasoning
Pistachios	Button	Chilli powder

	mushrooms	
Cottage cheese	Frozen spinach	Roma tomatoes
Butter	Shredded mozzarella	Raw macadamia nuts
Heavy cream	Unsweetened flour	
Spinach	Dark chocolate	
Mushrooms	Almonds	
Green bell pepper	Vanilla essence	
Extra virgin olive oil	Granulated sweetener of your choice	
Brussel sprouts	Baking soda	

Week 1

Day 1	Total Count: Fat: 69.9 grams Carbohydrates: 36 grams Protein: 35.3 grams
Breakfast	**Baked Zucchini Parmigianino** Fat: 17.5 grams Carbohydrates: 13.8 grams Protein: 14.1 grams
Lunch	**Creamy Cheese Brussel Sprouts** Fat: 18.5 grams Carbohydrates: 11.7 grams Protein: 9.8 grams
Dinner	**Broiled Eggs** Fat: 20.9 grams Carbohydrates: 2.8 grams Protein: 8.5 grams
Dessert	**Almond Choco Brownie** Fat: 13 grams Carbohydrates: 7.7 grams Protein: 2.9 grams
Day 2	Total Count: Fat: 117.8 grams Carbohydrates: 35.4 grams Protein: 25.4 grams
Breakfast	**Flax Meal Cinnamon Porridge** Fat: 10.5 grams Carbohydrates: 6 grams Protein: 3.4 grams

Lunch	**Greens and Red Hot Salad** Fat: 7.3 grams Carbohydrates: 13.4 grams Protein: 7.3 grams
Dinner	**Cheesy Fried Eggplant Slices** Fat: 33 grams Carbohydrates: 7.9 grams Protein: 13.2 grams
Dessert	**Carrot Coconut Muffins** Fat: 8.1 grams Carbohydrates: 8.1 grams Protein: 1.5 grams
Day 3	**Total Count:** Fat: 33.6 grams Carbohydrates: 24.8 grams Protein: 28 grams
Breakfast	**Feta Minty Omelet** Fat: 7.6 grams Carbohydrates: 0.8 grams Protein: 9.9 grams
Lunch	**Spinach Puree and Swiss Chard** Fat: 2.8 grams Carbohydrates: 8.7 grams Protein: 3 grams
Dinner	**Egg with Power Greens and Sweet Potato Casserole** Fat: 11.9 grams Carbohydrates: 10.8 grams Protein: 13.8 grams

Dessert	**Pumpkin Ice-cream** Fat: 11.3 grams Carbohydrates: 4.5 grams Protein: 1.3 grams
Day 4	**Total Count:** Fat: 49 grams Carbohydrates: 22.8 grams Protein: 26.3 grams
Breakfast	**Flaxseed Savory Waffles** Fat: 16 grams Carbohydrates: 1.5 grams Protein: 5.2 grams
Lunch	**Basil Zucchini Noodles** Fat: 15.6 grams Carbohydrates: 5.6 grams Protein: 3.9 grams
Dinner	**Mushrooms Roasted With Herbs & Parmesan** Fat: 9.7 grams Carbohydrates: 5.3 grams Protein: 14.8 grams
Dessert	**Strawberry Gateau** Fat: 7.7 grams Carbohydrates: 10.4 grams Protein: 2.4 grams
Day 5	**Total Count:** Fat: 37.7 grams Carbohydrates: 27 grams Protein: 27.6 grams
Breakfast	**Cauliflower Mozzarella Sticks** Fat: 13.9 grams Carbohydrates: 6.7 grams

	Protein: 21.7 grams
Lunch	**Sour Braised Artichokes** Fat: 5.6 grams Carbohydrates: 14.5 grams Protein: 4.3 grams
Dinner	**Roasted Sweet Potatoes and Cardamom** Fat: 6.9 grams Carbohydrates: 1.3 grams Protein: 0.3 grams
Dessert	**Pumpkin Pie** Fat: 11.3 grams Carbohydrates: 4.5 grams Protein: 1.3 grams
Day 6	**Total Count:** Fat: 29.4 grams Carbohydrates: 36.4 grams Protein: 20.9 grams
Breakfast	**Pistachio Leek Muffins** Fat: 7.4 grams Carbohydrates: 8 grams Protein: 4.9 grams
Lunch	**Mushroom and Broccoli Mix** Fat: 3.5 grams Carbohydrates: 10.9 grams Protein: 12.7 grams
Dinner	**Lemon Green Beans & Caper Vinaigrette** Fat: 10.4 grams Carbohydrates: 8.7 grams Protein: 1.8 grams

Dessert	**Carrot Muffins** Fat: 8.1 grams Carbohydrates: 8.8 grams Protein: 1.5 grams
Day 7	**Total Count:** Fat: 63.5 grams Carbohydrates: 25.1 grams Protein: 59.7 grams
Breakfast	**Flaxseed Cottage Pancakes** Fat: 13 grams Carbohydrates: 4.5 grams Protein: 6.1 grams
Lunch	**Bok Choy Warm Salad** Fat: 3.5 grams Carbohydrates: 10.9 grams Protein: 12.7 grams
Dinner	**Garlic Scallops** Fat: 34 grams Carbohydrates: 2 grams Protein: 38 grams
Dessert	**Almond Choco Brownie** Fat: 13 grams Carbohydrates: 7.7 grams Protein: 2.9 grams

Week 2

Day 1	**Total Count:** Fat: 48.8 grams Carbohydrates: 28.8 grams Protein: 34 grams
Breakfast	**Flaxseed Cottage Pancakes** Fat: 13 grams Carbohydrates: 4.5 grams Protein: 6.1 grams
Lunch	**Bok Choy Warm Salad** Fat: 10.1 grams Carbohydrates: 9.9 grams Protein: 8.5 grams
Dinner	**Crustless, Feta Mushroom Quiche** Fat: 18 grams Carbohydrates: 4 grams Protein: 17 grams
Dessert	**Strawberry Gateau** Fat: 7.7 grams Carbohydrates: 10.4 grams Protein: 2.4 grams
Day 2	**Total Count** Fat: 53 grams Carbohydrates: 29.7 grams Protein: 57.1 grams
Breakfast	**Pistachio and Leek Muffins** Fat: 7.4 grams Carbohydrates: 8 grams Protein: 4.9 grams

Lunch	**Mushroom & Broccoli Mix** Fat: 3.5 grams Carbohydrates: 10.9 grams Protein: 12.7 grams
Dinner	**Garlic Scallops** Fat: 34 grams Carbohydrates: 2 grams Protein: 38 grams
Dessert	**Carrot Coconut Muffins** Fat: 8.1 grams Carbohydrates: 8.8 grams Protein: 1.5 grams
Day 3	**Total Count:** Fat: 42.9 grams Carbohydrates: 45.3 grams Protein: 30.7 grams
Breakfast	**Cauliflower Mozzarella Sticks** Fat: 13.9 grams Carbohydrates: 6.7 grams Protein: 21.7 grams
Lunch	**Sour Braised Artichokes** Fat: 5.6 grams Carbohydrates: 14.5 grams Protein: 4.3 grams
Dinner	**Lemon Green Beans & Caper Vinaigrette** Fat: 10.4 gram Carbohydrates: 8.7 grams Protein: 1.8 grams

Dessert	**Almond Choco Brownie** Fat: 13 grams Carbohydrates: 7.7 grams Protein: 2.9 grams
Day 4	**Total Count:** Fat: 46.2 grams Carbohydrates: 18.8 grams Protein: 18.4 grams
Breakfa st	**Flaxseed Savory Waffles** Fat: 16 grams Carbohydrates: 1.5 grams Protein: 5.2 grams
Lunch	**Basil Zucchini Noodles** Fat: 15.6 grams Carbohydrates: 5.6 grams Protein: 3.9 grams
Dinner	**Roasted Sweet Potatoes and Cardamom** Fat: 6.9 grams Carbohydrates: 1.3 grams Protein: 6.9 grams
Dessert	**Strawberry Gateau** Fat: 7.7 grams Carbohydrates: 10.4 grams Protein: 2.4 grams
Day 5	**Total Count** Fat: 31.4 grams Carbohydrates: 38.6 grams Protein: 29 grams

Breakfast	**Feta Minty Omelet** Fat: 7.6 grams Carbohydrates: 0.8 grams Protein: 9.9 grams
Lunch	**Spinach Puree and Swiss Chard** Fat: 2.8 grams Carbohydrates: 8.7 grams Protein: 3 grams
Dinner	**Mushrooms Roasted With Herbs & Parmesan** Fat: 9.7 grams Carbohydrates: 5.3 grams Protein: 14.8 grams
Dessert	**Pumpkin Ice-cream** Fat: 11.3 grams Carbohydrates: 4.5 grams Protein: 1.3 grams
Day 6	**Total Count:** Fat: 37.8 grams Carbohydrates: 39 grams Protein: 25.2 grams
Breakfast	**Flax Meal Cinnamon Porridge** Fat: 10.5 grams Carbohydrates: 6 grams Protein: 3.4 grams
Lunch	**Greens and Red Hot Salad** Fat: 7.3 grams Carbohydrates: 13.4 grams Protein: 6.5 grams

Dinner	**Egg with Power Greens and Sweet Potato Casserole** Fat: 11.9 grams Carbohydrates: 10.8 grams Protein: 13.8 grams
Dessert	**Carrot Coconut Muffins** Fat: 8.1 grams Carbohydrates: 8.8 grams Protein: 1.5 grams
Day 7	**Total Count:** Fat: 82 grams Carbohydrates: 41.1 grams Protein: 40 grams
Breakfast	**Baked Zucchini Parmigianino** Fat: 17.5 grams Carbohydrates: 13.8 grams Protein: 14.1 grams
Lunch	**Creamy Cheese Brussel Sprouts** Fat: 18.5 grams Carbohydrates: 11.7 grams Protein: 9.8 grams
Dinner	**Cheesy Fried Eggplant Slices** Fat: 33 grams Carbohydrates: 7.9 grams Protein: 13.2 grams
Dessert	**Almond Choco Brownie** Fat: 13 grams Carbohydrates: 7.7 grams Protein: 2.9 grams

Chapter 4: Delicious Breakfasts

1: Baked Zucchini Parmigianino
(Prep time: 40 minutes/6 servings)

Ingredients

- 3 large eggs
- 1 cup of almond flour
- 1 cup of ground almonds
- 2 zucchinis, thinly sliced
- 1 cup of Parmigiano-Reggiano grated
- 1 teaspoon of dried oregano
- Salt and pepper

Preparation

1. Preheat oven to 400°F. Line a large baking dish with parchment paper.
2. In a large bowl combine the oregano, Parmigiano-Reggiano cheese, season with salt and pepper. Set aside.
3. Pour the almond flour in a separate bowl.
4. In another bowl, whisk the eggs together. Add salt and pepper.

5. Dip sliced zucchini in flour, then in egg mixture, then in ground almond mixture.
6. Place zucchini slices in a single layer on the baking tray. Bake 30 minutes. Serve.

Nutrition Values

- Carbohydrates: 13.8 grams
- Fat: 17.5 grams
- Protein: 14.1 grams

2: Flax Meal Cinnamon Porridge
(Prep time: 5 minutes/ 1 serving)

Ingredients

- 4 Tablespoons of soft cream cheese
- 4 Tablespoons of flax meal
- 1 cup of water
- 1 cup of sweetener
- Ground cinnamon

Preparation

1. Add listed ingredients to a microwave safe bowl. Stir well.
2. Microwave for 2 minutes. Stir again. Top with fresh berries.
3. Serve.

Nutritional Value

- Carbohydrates: 6 grams
- Fat: 10.5 grams
- Protein: 3.4 grams

3: Feta Minty Omelette
(Prep time: 15 minutes/2 servings)

Ingredients

- 3 large eggs
- 6 mint leaves
- 4 ounces of feta cheese
- Salt and pepper
- Olive oil

Preparation

1. Preheat oven to 400°F.
2. In a medium bowl, combine eggs and feta cheese, mint leaves, salt and pepper. Whisk thoroughly.
3. In a non-stick, oven-safe frying pan, heat up some olive oil (light layer drizzled over bottom). Pour the egg mixture in frying pan. Cook for 3 minutes.
4. Remove frying pan from stove, place in oven. Cook 5 minutes.
5. Transfer omelette to a plate. Serve.

Nutrition Value

- Carbohydrates: 0.8 grams
- Fat: 7.6 grams
- Protein: 9.9 grams

4: Flaxseed Savoury Waffles
(Prep time: 15 minutes/6 servings)

Ingredients

- 5 large eggs
- 2 cups of ground flaxseed
- 1 Tablespoon baking powder (gluten-free)
- ½ teaspoon sea salt
- 1 cup of water
- ½ cup of melted coconut oil
- 1 Tablespoon fresh herbs (sage, cilantro, parsley, basil)

Preparation

1. Pre-heat waffle maker to medium heat.
2. In a large bowl, combine baking powder, salt, and flaxseed. Whisk thoroughly.
3. In a separate bowl, add eggs, oil and water. Use handheld mixer, blend until fully combined. Pour egg mixture in with flaxseed mixture. Stir together. Let it rest 5 minutes. Add the fresh herbs. Stir well.
4. Pour ¼ cup of mixture onto waffle maker. Cook 3 – 5 minutes.

5. Serve.

Nutritional Value

- Carbohydrates: 1.5 grams
- Fats: 16 grams
- Protein: 5.2 grams

5: Cauliflower Mozzarella Sticks

(Prep time: 50 minutes/6 Servings)

Ingredients

- 4 cups of cauliflower rice
- 2 cups + 1 cup of mozzarella cheese
- 4 large eggs
- 4 cloves of minced garlic
- 3 teaspoons of fresh oregano
- Salt and pepper

Instructions

1. Preheat oven to 400°F.
2. Rinse cauliflower, pat dry. Cut into florets.
3. Place florets in food processor. Pulse until rice-like consistency.
4. Transfer cauliflower to microwavable container. Cover and cook 10 minutes.
5. Pour cauliflower into a large bowl. Add the 2 cups of mozzarella cheese, eggs, oregano, salt, pepper and garlic. Stir together.
6. Line two large baking trays with parchment paper. Spread mixture in

single even layer on the baking trays. Bake 25 minutes, until golden brown.

7. Remove trays from oven. Sprinkle remaining cup of mozzarella cheese over cauliflower. Return to oven for 5 minutes, until cheese melts.

8. Remove from oven. Let it rest for 5 minutes. Slice into sticks.

9. Side with marinara sauce. Serve.

Nutritional Value

- Carbohydrates: 6.7 grams
- Fat: 13.9 grams
- Protein: 21.7 grams

6: Pistachio and Leek Muffins
(Prep time: 40 minutes/12 Servings)

Ingredients

- 1 cup of millet flour
- ½ cup of tapioca flour
- 1 teaspoon of baking powder
- 3 Tablespoons of olive oil
- 1½ cups of milk
- 2 large eggs
- 2 leeks, chopped and washed
- ½ cup of chopped pistachios

Instructions

1. Preheat oven to 400°F. Line muffin tin with paper liners.
2. In a large bowl, combine baking powder, flour and salt. Whisk thoroughly.
3. In a separate bowl, combine milk, eggs, and oil. Whisk thoroughly.
4. Pour egg mixture into flour mixture. Stir until combined.
5. Add half the pistachios and leeks. Stir well.

6. Fill muffin cup ¾ full. Sprinkle rest of chopped pistachios over top.
7. Bake 25 minutes, until golden brown. Cool for 15 minutes. Serve.

Nutritional Value

- Carbohydrates: 8 grams
- Fat: 7.4 grams
- Protein: 4.9 grams

7: Flaxseed Cottage Pancakes
(Prep time: 15 minutes/6 Servings)

Ingredients

- ½ cup of ground flax seed meal
- 3 Tablespoons of cottage cheese
- 2 large eggs
- 2 Tablespoons of butter
- ½ cup of heavy cream
- ¼ teaspoon of gluten-free baking powder
- Coconut oil or olive oil for frying

Instructions

1. In a large bowl combine all the ingredients. Whisk together thoroughly
2. In a non-stick frying pan, heat the oil.
3. Spoon ¾ cup of batter onto frying pan. Cook 2 minutes per side.
4. Transfer onto plate. Serve with fresh berries or (keto-friendly) syrup.

Nutritional Value

- Carbohydrates: 4.5 grams
- Fat: 13 grams
- Protein: 6.1 grams

8: Baked Eggs With Spinach and Mushrooms
(Prep time: 20 minutes/3 Servings)

Ingredients

- 4 large eggs
- 3 cups of chopped spinach
- 3 cups of sliced mushrooms
- 1 coarsely chopped green bell pepper
- 2 Tablespoons of extra virgin olive oil
- Salt and pepper

Instructions

1. Preheat oven to 400°F. Grease 8x8 baking dish with olive oil.
2. Place bell peppers, spinach, and mushrooms in baking dish.
3. Carefully crack the eggs over the vegetables. Season with salt and pepper.
4. Bake until the whites are set, approximately 10 minutes.
5. Remove from oven. Transfer to plates. Serve.

Nutritional Value

- Carbohydrates: 7.6 grams
- Fat: 9.9 grams
- Protein: 12.7 grams

Chapter 5: Flavorful Lunches

9: Creamy Cheese Brussel Sprouts
(Prep time: 15 minutes/2 Servings)

Ingredients

- 25 Brussel sprouts
- 4 cloves of garlic, minced
- ¾ cup of cream cheese
- 2 Tablespoons of extra virgin olive oil
- 2 teaspoons of organic fresh lemon juice
- Salt and pepper

Preparation

1. Rinse Brussel sprouts in cold water. Remove stem.
2. Heat olive oil in non-stick frying pan.
3. Add minced garlic and Brussel sprouts. Sauté until tender.
4. Stir in cream cheese and lemon juice.
5. Transfer to bowls. Serve.

Nutritional Value

- Carbohydrates: 11.7 grams
- Fat: 18.5 grams
- Protein: 9.8 grams

10: Greens and Red Hot Salad
(Prep time: 15 minutes/6 Servings)

Ingredients

- 1½ pounds of red cabbage, sliced into small wedges
- 1½ pounds of Brussel sprouts, sliced into small wedges
- 3 medium beets, sliced into small wedges
- 8 cloves of garlic, minced
- 3 Tablespoons of olive oil
- 1 Tablespoon of finely chopped fresh thyme

Instructions

1. Place chopped vegetables and garlic in pressure cooker.
2. Add the salt, pepper, thyme, and oil. Stir.
3. Set the cooker on Sauté. Cook for 15 minutes on high pressure.
4. Once ready, select natural release. Allow pressure to go down naturally. (Approximately 15 - 20 minutes.)
5. Transfer vegetables to a platter. Serve.

Nutritional Values

- Carbohydrates: 13.4 grams
- Fat: 7.3 grams
- Protein: 6.5 grams

11: Spinach Puree and Swiss Chard
(Prep time: 25 minutes/8 servings)

Ingredients

- ½ pound of swiss chard
- 1 pound of baby spinach leaves
- 1 cup of cauliflower florets
- 1 leek
- 4 Tablespoons of extra virgin olive oil
- 3 cups of water
- ¼ cup of cream cheese
- Salt and pepper

Instructions

1. Rinse the leek. Dice into thick slices.
2. Heat olive oil in non-stick frying pan. Add cauliflower and leek. Cook for 3 minutes.
3. Add spinach leaves, swiss chard, salt and pepper. Simmer 15 minutes.
4. Allow vegetables to cool down 10 minutes. Transfer to food processor. Blend into a soup. Return to the stove. Stir in cream cheese and water. Heat 5 minutes.

5. Pour into bowls. Serve.

Nutritional Value

- Carbohydrates: 8.7 grams
- Fat: 2.8 grams
- Protein: 3 grams

12: Basil Zucchini Noodles
(Prep time: 15 minutes/3 Servings)

Ingredients

- 3 Tablespoons of chopped fresh basil
- 2 cups of zucchini noodles
- 4 Tablespoons of extra virgin olive oil
- 4 cloves of garlic, mashed
- 1 teaspoon of red pepper flakes
- ½ bell red pepper, chopped
- Salt and pepper

Instructions

1. Use a spiralizer to turn zucchini into noodles.
2. Heat olive oil in non-stick frying pan. Add garlic, red pepper flakes, red pepper. Sauté for 1-2 minutes, until garlic releases aroma.
3. Add zucchini noodles. Stir well. Cook 3 minutes.
4. Transfer zucchini noodle mix to a plate. Garnish with basil. Serve.

Nutritional Values

- Carbohydrates: 5.6 grams
- Fat: 15.6 grams
- Protein: 3.9 grams

13: Sour Braised Artichokes
(Prep time: 2-4 hours/4 Servings)

Ingredients

- 4 artichokes
- 4 Tablespoons of lemon juice
- 2 Tablespoons of melted coconut butter
- Water
- Salt and pepper
- Fresh chopped thyme

Instructions

1. Rinse artichokes and trim. Remove leaves until light yellow leaves are left. Slice off top third of artichoke, trim end of the stem.
2. Place artichokes, lemon juice, melted coconut butter and salt in slow cooker.
3. Cover and cook on high 2 hours, or low 4 hours, until artichokes are fork tender.
4. Transfer to platter. Garnish with chopped thyme. Serve.

Nutritional Value

- Carbohydrates: 14.5 grams
- Fat: 5.6 grams
- Protein: 4.3 grams

14: Mushroom & Broccoli Mix
(Prep time: 35 minutes/2 Servings)

Ingredients

- 2 cups of thinly sliced button mushrooms
- 4 cups of broccoli
- 2 Tablespoons of minced garlic
- ½ teaspoon of dried oregano
- 4 Tablespoons of grated Parmesan
- Salt and pepper

Instructions

1. Preheat oven to 400°F. Line medium baking dish with parchment paper.
2. In a large bowl, combine mushrooms and broccoli. Coat with olive oil.
3. Season with salt, pepper, and oregano.
4. Transfer broccoli and mushrooms to baking dish. Bake 25 minutes.
5. Serve.

Nutritional Values

- Carbohydrates: 10.9 grams
- Fats: 3.5 grams
- Protein: 12.7 grams

15: Bok Choy Warm Salad
(Prep time: 10 minutes/3 servings)

Ingredients

- 1 bunch of trimmed bok choy
- 2 cups of water
- 2 Tablespoons of olive oil
- 2 Tablespoons of fresh-squeezed lime juice
- Salt and pepper

Instructions

1. Place bok choy in pressure cooker. Add enough water to cover.
2. Close lid. Set pressure on high. Cook 7 minutes.
3. Once cooked, allow pressure to drop naturally, approximately 20 minutes.
4. Transfer to serving platter. Drizzle lime juice and oil over. Sprinkle salt and pepper. Serve.

Nutritional Value

- Carbohydrates: 9.9 grams
- Fat: 10.1 grams
- Protein: 8.5 grams

16: Asparagus and Artichoke Salad
(Prep time: 1 hour and 5 minutes/8 servings)

Ingredients

- 20 tender, fresh green asparagus (woodsy stem removed, rinsed)
- 8 fresh, medium artichokes
- 4 Tablespoons of extra virgin olive oil
- 2 cloves of garlic, peeled and chopped
- 1 ounce of chopped pistachio nuts
- 1 large egg white
- 4 teaspoons of chopped green onions + 1 green onion for garnish, chopped
- Juice from 1 lemon
- Salt and white pepper

Instructions

1. In a large pot, fill to ¾, add juice from half the lemon and sprinkle of salt.
2. Peel off leaves from the artichoke. Set hearts aside. Place artichoke leaves in boiling water. Cook 45 minutes. Once boiled, rinse under cold water.

3. Place in food processor. Add rest of lemon juice, half a glass of water, pinch of salt and pepper, pistachios, green onions, garlic, and egg white. Blend for 1 minute. Add olive oil slowly. Continue to blend until medium consistency.

4. Cut up artichoke hearts and arrange on plate. Place asparagus over top. Drizzle sauce over artichokes and asparagus. Garnish with fresh green onions. Serve.

Nutritional Value

- Carbohydrates: 11 grams
- Fat: 7 grams
- Protein 5.9 grams

Chapter 6: Mouth-Watering Dinners

17: Broiled Eggs
(Prep time: 20 minutes/2 servings)

Ingredients

- 4 large eggs
- 6 Tablespoons of heavy cream
- 1 Tablespoon of extra virgin olive oil
- 1 Tablespoon of parmesan cheese
- ¼ cup button mushrooms, sliced
- ¼ cup of baby spinach
- 1 pinch of red pepper flakes
- Salt and pepper

Instructions

1. Preheat broiler to 400°F. Rinse mushrooms, pat dry.
2. In a large non-stick, oven-safe frying pan, heat the oil. Fry the eggs on one side for 3 minutes. Set eggs aside for the moment.

3. Pour half the heavy cream in the pan. Add mushrooms. Simmer for 3 minutes.
4. Stir in rest of heavy cream. Add Parmesan cheese. Stir well.
5. Place under broiler 3 minutes.
6. Pull pan out of oven. Add spinach leaves and red pepper flakes. Stir well.
7. Return eggs to the pan. Place pan under broiler 2-3 minutes.
8. Pull pan from oven. Sprinkle parmesan cheese over top.
9. Garnish with fresh spinach leaves. Serve.

Nutritional Value

- Carbohydrates: 2.8 grams
- Fat: 20.9 grams
- Protein: 8.5 grams

18: Cheesy Fried Eggplant Slices
(Prep time: 20 minutes/6 servings)

Ingredients

- 1 eggplant
- 1 large egg
- 1 cup of almond flour
- 1 cup of grated Parmesan cheese
- ½ cup of coconut oil or butter
- Garlic powder
- Salt and pepper

Instructions

1. Rinse the eggplant, pat dry. Slice in ½ inch thickness. Arrange on a plate.
2. Sprinkle with salt. Let sit for 30 minutes.
3. In a small bowl, whisk the egg. In a separate bowl, combine Parmesan cheese, garlic powder, almond flour, salt and pepper. Stir well.
4. Heat butter or oil in a non-stick frying pan over medium heat.
5. Dip slice of eggplant in egg, then flour. Fry until crispy and golden brown.

6. Place cooked eggplant on a paper towel lined plate to drain excess oil.
7. Serve.

Nutritional Value

- Carbohydrates: 7.9 grams
- Fat: 33 grams
- Protein: 13.2 grams

19: Egg with Power Greens and Sweet Potato Casserole

(Prep time: 1 hour and 10 minutes/4 Servings)

Ingredients

- 8 large eggs
- ½ teaspoon of coconut oil
- 4 cups of power greens (spinach, kale, arugula)
- 2 peeled sweet potatoes, diced
- 1 diced green onion
- ¼ cup of coconut milk
- 1 teaspoon of garlic powder
- ¼ teaspoon of nutmeg
- Salt and pepper
- Seasoning of your choice

Instructions

1. Preheat oven to 400°F. Grease casserole dish with coconut oil.
2. In a large bowl, whisk eggs. Add onions, sweet potato, coconut milk, power greens and seasoning. Pour egg mixture in dish.

3. Place dish in the oven. Bake 45 minutes.
4. Remove dish from the oven. Cover with foil. Bake 15 more minutes.
5. Remove from oven. Separate onto plates. Serve.

Nutritional Values

- Carbohydrates: 10.8 grams
- Fat: 11.9 grams
- Protein: 13.8 grams

20: Mushrooms Roasted With Herbs & Parmesan

(Prep time: 35 minutes/6 Servings)

Ingredients

- 1 pound of Cremini mushrooms
- 1 can of diced tomatoes
- 2 cups of grated Parmesan cheese
- 2 Tablespoons of ghee
- 2 Tablespoons of mashed garlic
- 1 Tablespoon of fresh parsley
- 2 Tablespoons of fresh basil
- 1 Tablespoon of fresh thyme
- Salt and pepper

Instructions

1. Preheat the oven to 400°F. Rinse the mushrooms, pat dry. Slice off stems.
2. In a large non-stick, oven-safe frying pan, melt the ghee.
3. Sauté the mushrooms for 5 minutes. Season with salt and pepper.

4. In a medium bowl, combine the herbs, tomatoes, salt and pepper. Stir mixture in with mushrooms. Sprinkle Parmesan cheese over top. Bake 25 minutes.
5. Remove from oven. Divide on plates. Serve.

Nutritional Values

- Carbohydrates: 5.3 grams
- Fat: 9.7 grams
- Protein: 14.8 grams

21: Roasted Sweet Potatoes and Cardamom

(Prep time: 1 hour 10 minutes/4 Servings)

Ingredients

- 2½ pounds of sweet potatoes
- 2 Tablespoons of softened coconut butter
- ½ teaspoon of ground cardamom
- 4 chopped green onions
- Handful of shallots
- Salt and white pepper
- Olive oil

Instructions

1. Preheat the oven to 400°F.
2. Heat coconut butter in large non-stick, oven-safe frying pan over medium heat. Sautee onions for 4 minutes. Season with salt and pepper.
3. Peel the potatoes, dice into cubes. Place in a medium bowl.
4. Peel the shallots, add to potatoes. Add cardamom and butter. Stir. Season with

salt and pepper. Add ingredients to oven-safe frying pan.

5. Bake until tender, approximately 1 hour. Serve.

Nutritional Values

- Carbohydrates: 1.3 grams
- Fat: 6.9 grams
- Protein: 0.3 grams

22: Lemon Green Beans & Caper Vinaigrette

(Prep time: 15 minutes/4 Servings)

Ingredients

- 1 pound of trimmed fresh green beans
- 3 Tablespoons of olive oil
- 2 Tablespoons of chopped capers
- Zest and juice from 1 lemon
- Salt and pepper

Instructions

1. In a large bowl, whisk the lemon juice, capers, oil, salt and pepper.
2. Boil a large pot of water, add 1 tablespoon of salt. Cook the green beans until tender, approximately 4-6 minutes.
3. Drain the beans. Rinse in cold water.
4. Drizzle caper vinaigrette over beans, toss to coat. Transfer to plates. Serve.

Nutritional Values

- Carbohydrates: 8.7 grams
- Fat: 10.4 grams
- Protein: 1.8 grams

23: Garlic Scallops
(Prep time: 10 minutes /2 Servings)

Ingredients

- 1 pound of large scallop
- ¼ cup of clarified ghee butter
- 5 cloves of grated garlic
- 1 large lemon
- Zest from 1 large lemon
- ¼ cup of roughly chopped Italian parsley
- Sea salt
- Black pepper
- ¼ teaspoon of red pepper flakes
- 1 pinch of sweet paprika
- 1 teaspoon of extra virgin olive oil

Instructions

1. Use paper towels to pat dry the scallops. Place in a medium bowl.
2. Coat with olive oil. Season with sweet paprika, red pepper flakes, black pepper and sea salt. Toss to coat evenly.

3. Heat a large frying pan on medium heat. Melt the ghee. Add the scallops. Cook 2 minutes per side, until golden brown.
4. Add garlic to frying pan. Take pan off stove. Stir ingredients for 30 seconds.
5. Squeeze half of the lemon juice over scallops. Sprinkle lemon zest, parsley and extra virgin olive oil over scallops. Stir.
6. Side with noodles or crusty bread. Serve.

Nutritional Values

- Carbohydrates: 2 grams
- Fat: 34 grams
- Protein: 38 grams

24: Crustless, Feta, Mushroom Quiche
(Prep time: 45 minutes / 6 Servings)

Ingredients

- 8 ounces of button mushrooms, thinly sliced
- 1 clove of garlic, minced
- 10 ounces of thawed frozen spinach
- 4 large eggs
- 1 cup of milk
- 2 ounces of feta cheese
- ¼ cup of grated Parmesan
- ½ cup of shredded mozzarella
- Salt & pepper

Instructions

1. Preheat oven to 400°F. Squeeze excess water out of thawed spinach.
2. Heat some cooking oil in a large non-stick frying pan over medium heat.
3. Add garlic and mushrooms. Sauté until tender, approximately 7 minutes.

4. Grease a large pie dish with non-stick spray. Arrange spinach along bottom of pie dish. Pour mushrooms and garlic over spinach. Crumble feta cheese over top.
5. In a large bowl, whisk together milk, eggs, and Parmesan cheese. Lightly season with pepper. Pour egg mixture on top of ingredients in pie dish.
6. Sprinkle mozzarella over the top.
7. Place pie dish on a baking tray. Place it into the oven. Bake for approximately 45 minutes, until golden brown.
8. Remove from oven. Let it rest for 5 minutes before slicing. Serve.

Nutritional Values

- Carbohydrates: 4 grams
- Fat: 18 grams
- Protein: 17 grams

Chapter 7: Amazing Desserts & Side Dishes

25: Almond Choco Brownies
(Prep time: 35 minutes/16 Servings)

Ingredients

- 3 large eggs
- 1 cup of almond flour
- 2 Tablespoons of unsweetened flour
- 4 ounces of dark chocolate
- ½ cup of melted coconut oil
- 1 cup of chopped almonds
- 1 teaspoon of vanilla essence
- 2 cups of any granulated sweetener
- 1 teaspoon of baking soda
- Salt

Instructions

1. Preheat oven to 400°F. Line an 8x8 baking dish with parchment paper.
2. Place the dark chocolate in a microwaveable bowl and microwave for 15 seconds.

3. To melt the coconut oil, place the bottom of the jar into a bowl of boiling water.
4. Combine the coconut oil and the melted chocolate in a bowl. Stir gently until combined. Set aside. It needs to cool before adding it to anything with eggs.
5. In a deep bowl combine the cocoa powder, sweetener, baking soda, salt, and almond flour. Stir until mixed.
6. Start your handheld mixer on slow. Add the eggs one at a time to the flour mixture. Add the vanilla essence to the flour mixture. Blend until combined.
7. Pour the chocolate mixture into the batter. Blend for 1 minute. Add the almonds. Stir by hand to mix in.
8. Pour batter into baking dish. Bake for 25 minutes.
9. Once cooked, allow to cool at least 30 minutes before slicing.
10. Serve.

Nutritional Values

- Carbohydrates: 7.7 grams
- Fat: 13 grams
- Protein: 2.9 grams

26: Carrot Coconut Muffins
(Prep time: 50 minutes/12 Servings)

Ingredients

- ¼ cup of coconut flour
- 1 teaspoon of baking powder
- 2 cups of shredded carrots
- 2 large eggs
- ½ cup of coconut oil
- 1 teaspoon of vanilla extract
- ¼ cup of any sweetener
- 2 teaspoons of ground cinnamon

Instructions

1. Preheat oven to 400°F. Line a 12 muffin tin with paper liners.
2. In a bowl, combine the coconut flour. Baking powder. Sweetener, cinnamon.
3. Add vanilla, sweetener, coconut oil, carrots and eggs to food processor. Blend until combined. Pour into dry ingredients. Stir until combined. (Don't overmix.)
4. Pour batter in each tin to ⅔ full.

5. Bake 35 minutes.
6. Allow to cool 30 minutes. Serve.

Nutritional Value

- Carbohydrates: 8.8 grams
- Fat: 8.1 grams
- Protein: 1.5 grams

27: Pumpkin Ice-cream
(Prep time: 15 minutes/6 Servings)

Ingredients

- 1 can of coconut milk
- 1 cup of unsweetened almond milk
- 1 cup of canned or fresh pumpkin puree
- 1 teaspoon of pure vanilla extract
- ½ teaspoon of nutmeg
- 2½ teaspoons of ground cinnamon
- ½ teaspoon of ground ginger
- Pinch of salt
- 1 Tablespoon of gelatin

Instructions

1. Dissolve gelatin in ¼ cup boiling water.
2. Add rest of ingredients, including gelatin, to food processor. Blend until smooth.
3. Transfer mixture to a freezer-safe container. Cover. Freeze for 2 hours.
4. After 2 hours, use a wooden spoon to stir the ice-cream, to prevent crystalizing.

5. Leave in freezer overnight. Serve the following day.

Nutritional Values

- Carbohydrates: 4.5 grams
- Fat: 11.3 grams
- Protein: 1.3 grams

28: Strawberry Gateau
(Prep time: 35 minutes/6 Servings)

Ingredients

- 4 large egg yolks
- 2 Tablespoons of butter
- 2 Tablespoons of coconut oil
- ¼ cup of coconut flour
- 2 Tablespoons of heavy cream
- ¼ cup of strawberries
- ¼ teaspoon of baking powder
- 2 teaspoons of lemon juice
- Zest from 1 lemon
- 2 Tablespoons of any granulated sweetener
- 10 drops of any liquid sweetener

Instructions

1. Preheat oven to 400∘F. Line an 8x8 baking dish with parchment paper.
2. In a small bowl, combine the egg yolks.
3. Using a handheld mixer, whisk until pale and fluffy.

4. Add liquid sweetener and granulated sweetener. Whisk until fully combined.
5. Add heavy cream, butter, coconut oil, lemon juice, lemon zest. Whisk until smooth.
6. Add baking soda and coconut flour. Continue to whisk until combined.
7. Add the strawberries. Stir gently.
8. Transfer batter to baking dish. Bake 25 minutes.
9. Allow to cool 30 minutes before slicing. Serve.

Nutritional Values

- Carbohydrates: 10.4 grams
- Fat: 7.7 grams
- Protein: 2.4 grams

29: Beetroot and Mustard Chips
(Prep time: 45 minutes/4 Servings)

Ingredients

- 5 beets
- 2 Tablespoons of olive oil
- 2 pinches of ground mustard seeds
- Salt and pepper

Instructions

1. Preheat oven to 400°F. Grease 2 baking sheets with olive oil.
2. Peel and slice the beets thinly using a mandolin, or the wide angle on a (cheese) grater. Place beets in a bowl.
3. Toss with olive oil. Season with mustard seeds, salt and pepper.
4. Arrange beets in single layer on baking sheets. Bake 40 minutes, or become crispy.
5. Cool 5 minutes before serving.

Nutritional Values

- Carbohydrates: 10.4 grams
- Fat: 7.1 grams
- Protein: 1.8 grams

30: Roasted Kale Chips
(Prep time: 20 minutes/3 Servings)

Ingredients

- 3 cups of chopped kale, throw away the stems
- 2 Tablespoons of extra virgin olive oil
- Salt and pepper

Instructions

1. Preheat the oven to 400°F. Line a baking tray with parchment paper.
2. Place the kale in a large bowl. Drizzle with olive oil. Season with salt and pepper.
3. Arrange the kale in single layer on baking tray.
4. Bake 12 minutes, until they become crispy.
5. Serve hot or cold.

Nutritional Values

- Carbohydrates: 10 grams
- Fat: 3.9 grams
- Protein: 2.5 grams

31: Parmesan Chips
(Prep time: 13 minutes/9 Servings)

Ingredients

- ¼ cup of shaved Parmesan
- ¼ cup of grated Parmesan
- Pinch of fresh ground pepper

Instructions

1. Preheat the oven to 400°F. Line 2 baking trays with parchment paper.
2. In a small bowl, combine the two cheeses and pepper. Stir well.
3. Using a teaspoon, spoon mixture on baking tray. Pat it down until almost flat. Leave about 1-2 inches space between piles. Repeat until you use all the mixture.
4. Bake in oven until golden brown and crispy, approximately 7 minutes.
5. Remove the baking tray from oven. Cool for 5 minutes before serving.

Nutritional Values

- Carbohydrates: 0 grams
- Fat: 3 grams
- Protein: 6 grams

32: Devilled Eggs

(Prep time: 25 minutes/ 10 Servings)

Ingredients

- 10 large eggs
- 4 Tablespoons of mayo
- 1 Tablespoon of Dijon mustard
- Splash of hot sauce
- Paprika seasoning

Instructions

1. Place the eggs in a large pot. Fill pot with water until eggs are covered.
2. Boil 15 minutes.
3. Once cooked, rinse under cold water. Peel and rinse in cold water.
4. Cut the eggs in half. Remove the yolks. Yolks in one bowl, whites on a plate.
5. Add hot sauce, mayo to egg yolks. Mash yolks with a fork. Stir until combined.
6. Spoon the yolk filling into hollowed egg whites, or fill a Ziploc baggie, cut a corner off, not too wide, and fill the eggs, with a

bump of egg yolk mixture above the white (as seen in picture).

7. Garnish with paprika seasoning. Refrigerate until ready to eat.

Nutritional Value

- Carbohydrates: 0.4 grams
- Fat: 9 grams
- Protein: 6 grams

Chapter 8: Soups

33: Cheesy Zucchini & Broccoli Soup
(Prep time: 45 minutes/4 Servings)

Ingredients

- 4 large green zucchinis
- 1 cup of broccoli, cut into small pieces
- 2 leeks (the white part)
- 3 Tablespoons of virgin olive oil
- 5 cups of water
- Salt and pepper
- Parmesan cheese

Instructions

1. In a large saucepan, heat the olive oil over medium heat. Add the leeks.
2. Cook until they are soft, stirring occasionally, approximately 10 minutes.
3. Add chopped broccoli and zucchinis. Sauté 5 minutes.
4. Add water. Simmer uncovered 15 minutes.

5. Using a handheld blender, blend the soup in the pot until smooth.
6. Transfer to bowls, sprinkle with cheese and serve.

Nutritional Value

- Carbohydrates: 11.7 grams
- Fat: 0.7 grams
- Protein: 3.4 grams

34: Garlic Castilian Soup
(Prep time: 35 minutes/6 Servings)

Ingredients

- 3 large cloves of garlic
- 2 Tablespoons of olive oil
- 3 cups of vegetable broth
- 3 cups of water
- 5 large eggs
- 1 thinly sliced red bell pepper
- Salt and pepper

Instructions

1. Heat the oil over medium heat in a large saucepan. Sauté the garlic 3 minutes.
2. Add 1 cup of vegetable broth. Cover and simmer 10 minutes.
3. Using a fork, mash the garlic into a paste.
4. Pour in water and rest of vegetable broth. Bring to a boil. Add the red pepper. Simmer 15 minutes. Break the eggs into the boiling soup.

5. Cook until the whites are solid, approximately 4 minutes. Serve immediately.

Nutritional Values

- Carbohydrates: 4.2 grams
- Fat: 9.3 grams
- Protein: 8.3 grams

35: Dill & Leek Soup
(Prep time: 35 minutes/6 Servings)

Ingredients

- 2 large green onions, chopped
- 2 large leeks
- 2 zucchini
- 2 cups of homemade vegetable broth
- 2 cups of water
- ¾ cup of heavy cream
- 2 Tablespoons of olive oil
- 1 Tablespoon of fresh dill, chopped
- Salt and pepper

Instructions

1. Wash the leeks. Remove dark green leaves. (Keep some dark leaves for garnish.)
2. Grate the green part of the zucchini.
3. Place the zucchini, green onions, leeks, water, and vegetable broth in a deep pot. Cover and simmer 20 minutes.

4. Allow to cool for 10 minutes. Pour ingredients in a blender. Blend for a few seconds.
5. Return the mixture to a pot. Stir in the heavy cream. Season with salt and pepper.
6. Spoon into bowls. Garnish with dark leaves from leeks. Serve.

Nutritional Value

- Carbohydrates: 11.3 grams
- Fat: 16.6 grams
- Protein: 3.9 grams

36: Grain-Free Vegan Mushroom Creamy Soup
(Prep time: 5 minutes/2 Servings)

Ingredients

- 2 cups of cauliflower florets
- 1½ cups of original almond milk unsweetened
- 1 teaspoon of onion powder
- ¼ teaspoon of Himalayan rock salt
- Ground black pepper
- ½ teaspoon of extra virgin olive oil
- 1½ cups of white button mushrooms, diced
- ½ yellow onion, diced
- Green onion for garnish, chopped

Instructions

1. In a medium saucepan, combine almond milk, cauliflower, salt, pepper and onion powder. Cover and simmer on medium heat 8 minutes, until cauliflower is tender.

Allow to cool for 5 minutes before pouring into food processor.
2. Transfer to food processor. Blend until smooth.
3. In a medium saucepan, heat some oil over medium heat. Sauté onions and mushrooms until they soften, approximately 6-8 minutes.
4. Pour cauliflower mixture in with onions and mushrooms. Cover and simmer 10 minutes. Soup will thicken. Garnish with fresh green onion. Serve while hot.

Nutritional Values

- Carbohydrates: 7.9 grams
- Fat: 4 grams
- Protein: 4.9 grams

37: Vegan Gazpacho
(Prep time: 6 minutes/6 Servings)

Ingredients

- 1 medium red onion, finely chopped
- 3 medium tomatoes, finely chopped
- ½ medium cucumber, finely chopped
- ½ green pepper, de-seeded, finely chopped
- 6 celery stalks, finely chopped celery stalks
- 1 clove of garlic, minced
- 3½ cups of tomato juice
- ¼ cup of extra virgin olive oil
- ¼ cup of white wine vinegar
- ¼ cup of fresh parsley, finely chopped
- ⅛ teaspoon of powdered white stevia
- Salt and pepper
- 1 batch of croutons

Instructions

1. Place all the ingredients in a large bowl. Stir together. Refrigerate 3 hours.

2. Serve in bowls. Garnish with croutons and fresh parsley.

Nutritional Value

- Carbohydrates: 16 grams
- Fat: 9 grams
- Protein: 2.9 grams

38: Vegan Creamy Broccoli Soup
(Prep time: 10 minutes/4 Servings)

Ingredients

- 1 Tablespoon of extra virgin olive oil
- 1 yellow onion, sliced
- 1 teaspoon of sea salt
- Ground black pepper
- 1 medium cauliflower, diced into florets
- 3 cups of unsweetened almond milk
- 3 cups broccoli florets
- 1 Tablespoon of onion powder

Instructions

1. In a large saucepan, heat the oil over medium heat. Sauté onions 5 minutes.
2. Add a few tablespoons of water while frying to make sure it doesn't burn.
3. Add milk and cauliflower. Season with salt and pepper.
4. Cover and simmer 10 minutes. Add half the broccoli. Cook 10 minutes. Allow to cool slightly before placing in food processor.

5. Transfer ingredients to food processor. Blend until smooth.
6. Pour ingredients in saucepan. Add onion powder and rest of the broccoli. Cover and cook 10 minutes, soup will thicken up. Spoon into bowls. Serve while hot.

Nutritional Values

- Carbohydrates: 19 grams
- Fat: 3.9 grams
- Protein: 6.5 grams

39: Mixed Greens Creamy Soup
(Prep time: 5 minutes/ 4 Servings)

Ingredients

- 2 cups of spinach leaves
- 1 avocado
- ½ cucumber
- 1 large green onion, chopped
- ½ cup of red bell peppers, chopped
- ¼ cup of gluten-free vegetable broth
- 1 clove of garlic, minced
- 1 Tablespoon of soy seasoning
- 1 Tablespoon of lemon juice
- 1 pinch of chilli powder
- Ground black pepper

Instructions

1. Transfer ingredients listed to a food processor. Blend 5 minutes, until smooth.
2. Pour into a medium saucepan. Cover and simmer 5 minutes. Serve in bowls.

Nutritional Values

- Carbohydrates: 6.7 grams
- Fat: 7.6 grams
- Protein: 2.1 grams

40: Tomato Soup
(Prep time: 5 minutes/ 4 Servings)

Ingredients

- 4 roma tomatoes
- ½ cup of sun dried tomatoes
- ½ cup of raw macadamia nuts
- 1 teaspoon of sea salt
- ¼ cup of fresh basil
- ½ teaspoon of black pepper
- 1 clove of garlic
- 4 cups of hot water

Instructions

1. Transfer ingredients listed to food processor. Blend 5 minutes, until smooth.
2. Pour into a medium saucepan. Cover and simmer 5 minutes. Serve in bowls.

Nutrition Values

- Carbohydrates: 11.8 grams
- Fat: 15.9 grams
- Protein: 3.5 grams

Conclusion

You made it to the end. Congratulations! I would like to thank you again for taking this journey of Ketogenic Vegetarian. I hope this book is helpful and you have found the information within the pages.

Keep in mind you are not limited to the recipes provided in this book. Continue exploring the vast choices available to you.

Stay healthy and stay safe!

Lightning Source UK Ltd.
Milton Keynes UK
UKOW01f1833161017
311091UK00009B/589/P